1 MONTH OF
FREE
READING

at

www.ForgottenBooks.com

By purchasing this book you are eligible for one month membership to ForgottenBooks.com, giving you unlimited access to our entire collection of over 1,000,000 titles via our web site and mobile apps.

To claim your free month visit:

www.forgottenbooks.com/free1121891

ISBN 978-0-331-42345-7
PIBN 11121891

This book is a reproduction of an important historical work. Forgotten Books uses
state-of-the-art technology to digitally reconstruct the work, preserving the original format
whilst repairing imperfections present in the aged copy. In rare cases, an imperfection in
the original, such as a blemish or missing page, may be replicated in our edition. We do,
however, repair the vast majority of imperfections successfully; any imperfections that
remain are intentionally left to preserve the state of such historical works.

PROCEEDINGS

OF THE

SIXTY-SIXTH ANNUAL SESSION

OF THE

WAKE BAPTIST ASSOCIATION

AND THE

FOURTEENTH ANNUAL SESSION

OF THE

WOMAN'S AUXILIARY

HELD WITH THE

FELTS CHAPEL BAPTIST CHURCH
NEAR YOUNGSVILLE, N. C.

REV. P. H. HEDGEPETH, Pastor

AUGUST 17-18, 1932

REV. M. W. WILLIAMS, Moderator
REV. GEORGE S. STOKES, Clerk

The next annual session will be held with the Olive Branch
Baptist Church, Wake Forest, N. C., Wednesday
before the third Sunday in August, 1933

OFFICERS

Moderator, Rev. M. W. Williams..Raleigh
Vice-Moderator, Rev. B. F. Jordan.......................................Wilson
Clerk, Rev. George S. Stokes..Middlesex
Corresponding Secretary, Rev. A. A. Morrissey..............Raleigh
Treasurer, Rev. C. C. Clark..Raleigh
Auditor, Rev. C. A. Marriott..Wendell
Statistician, ...

EXECUTIVE BOARD

Rev. M. W. Williams, Chairman; Rev. A. A. Morrissey, Rev. W. C. Somerville, Dr. N. F. Roberts, Rev. George S. Stokes, Rev. B. F. Jordan, Dr. O. S. Bullock, Rev. C. C. Clark, Rev. J. W. Jones, Rev. D. P. Lewis.

HOME MISSION BOARD

Rev. W. C. Somerville, Chairman; Rev. V. T. Williams, Dr. G. W. Moore, Rev. J. W. Powell, Rev. H. Y. Cheek, Rev. S. S. Hall, Rev. H. D. Eaton, Rev. C. C. Jones.

FOREIGN MISSION BOARD

Rev. Duffie Lewis, Chairman; Rev. C. A. Marriott, Rev. J. W. Powell, Rev. M. C. Ransom, Rev. P. H. Hedgepeth, Rev. J. F. Haywood, Rev. I. C. Jeffres, Bro. H. B. Cook.

EDUCATIONAL BOARD

Rev. A. B. Johnson, Chairman; Rev. C. F. Pope, Rev. C. C. Clark, Rev. J. H. Clanton, Dr. J. B. Davis, M.D., Rev. H. Y. Cheek.

SUNDAY SCHOOL BOARD

Rev. George S. Stokes, Chairman; Rev. G. W. Moore, Bro. Guyon Perry, Rev. M. W. Williams, Rev. W. T. Farror.

MINISTERIAL BOARD

Dr. N. F. Roberts, Chairman; Rev. J. L. Tilley, Rev. B. F. Jordan, Rev. N. A. Cheek, Rev. M. W. Williams, Rev. Geo. S. Stokes, Rev. V. T. Williams.

LIST OF ORDAINED MINISTERS

Rev. N. F. Roberts, D.D.........State College Station, Raleigh, N. C.

Rev. O. S. Bullock, D.D...... ....Raleigh, N. C.

Rev. Benjamin Brawley, Lit.D..........................Washington, D. C.

Rev. M. W. Williams, B.Th..Raleigh, N. C.

Rev. B. F. Jordan, B.Th... Wilson, N. C.

Rev. Geo. S. Stokes, A.B., B.Th....................... ......Middlesex, N. C.

Rev. J. L. Tilley, A.B., Ph.B............................ ...Raleigh, N. C.

Rev. C. C. Clark, B.S., B.Th............... ....Raleigh, N. C.

Rev. G. W. Watkins, D.D. ....Norfolk, Va.

Rev. A. A. Morrissey, B.Th....State College Station, Raleigh, N. C.

Rev. Jas. A. Pearce...Franklinton, N. C.

Rev. C. F. Pope, A.B., B.Th.... .... Raleigh, N. C.

Rev. N. W. Watkins............................... ....Franklinton, N. C.

Rev. Thomas Land ....Wake Forest, N. C.

Rev. J. W. Powell....................................Wake Forest, N. C.

Rev. S. S. Hall. ....Wendell, N. C.

Rev. M. W. Smith .. ..Wake Forest, N. C.

Rev. E. Wimberly..Durham, N. C.

Rev. Alvis Grady.... .. ..Hillsboro, N. C.

Rev. W. A. Cooper..................................... .. ..Hillsboro, N. C.

Rev. J. W. Carrington............................ ......Providence, R. I.

Rev. G. W. Todd. ....Smithfield, N. C.

Rev. Peter Alston................................. ....Henderson, N. C.

Rev. A. M. Wiggins..Middlesex, N. C.

Rev. J. A. Jones..............................R. 1, Knightdale, N. C.

Rev. E. W. Moragne..............1288 E. Edenton St., Raleigh, N. C.

Rev. E. C. Massenburg ....Wake Forest, N. C.

Rev. A. G. Seawell......................... ....Raleigh, N. C.

Rev. C. C. Jones.......................................Raleigh, N. C.

Rev. M. G. Watkins...Raleigh, N. C.

Rev. J. R. Dent.... ....Wake Forest, N. C.

Rev. J. F. Haywood.............. State College Station, Raleigh, N. C.

Rev. M. L. Dawson..................1111 Smithfield St., Raleigh, N. C.

Rev. H. D. Eaton, B.Th. ....Creedmoor, N. C.

Rev. W. M. Smith ....State College Station, Raleigh, N. C.

Rev. R. Crocket.......... .. .. Clayton, N. C.

Rev. J. W. Jones...... ....Wilson Mills, N. C.

Rev. L. E. Johnson.. ....Garner, N. C.

Rev. V. T. Williams.......................... ....Raleigh, N. C.

Rev. P. H. Hedgepeth.............................. Castalia, N. C.

Rev. G. W. Moore, D.D.............748 Fayetteville St., Raleigh, N. C.

Rev. W. H. Rogers..Zebulon, N. C.

Rev. J. H. Jones, A.B............................... ....Durham, N. C.

Rev. E. L. Crudup.................................... ....Bunn, N. C.

Rev. Wm. Perry .... Raleigh, N. C.
Rev. T. J. Foster .... Zebulon, N. C.
Rev. Chas. T. Jones .... Wilson, N. C.
Rev. A. B. Johnson, B.Th. .... Raleigh, N. C.
Rev. D. P. Lewis, A.B., B.Th. .... Louisburg, N. C.
Rev. Chas. P. Harris .... Franklinton, N. C.
Rev. W. T. Farror, B.Th. .... Franklinton, N. C.
Rev. W. C. Somerville, A.B., B.Th. .... Raleigh, N. C.
Rev. R. W. Daniel .... Franklinton, N. C.
Rev. W. H. Marable .... Wendell, N. C.
Rev. D. A. Thomas, B.S. .... Spring Hope, N. C.
Rev. Chas. A. Marriott, A.B. .... Wendell, N. C.
Rev. J. H. Williamson .... Louisburg, N. C.
Rev. Essex Henry, Jr. .... Raleigh, N. C.
Rev. N. A. Cheek .... Elberon, N. C.
Rev. J. H. Clanton, B.Th. .... Raleigh, N. C.
Rev. J. E. Marks, A.B. .... Raleigh, N. C.
Rev. H. Y. Cheek, A.B., B.Th. .... Henderson, N. C.
Rev. W. L. Wilson .... Louisburg, N. C.
Rev. A. A. Hartley .... Wilson Mills, N. C.
Rev. T. B. Smith .... McCullers, N. C.

LICENTIATE MINISTERS

Bethlehem, Jno. Lockley; Elevation, G. T. Bridges; Elizabeth, Felt's Chapel, S. M. Lucas, Joe Harris; First Baptist, Franklinton, H. B. Cook, J. H. Cook; First Baptist, Raleigh, T. E. Copland, G. F. Donald; First Baptist, Wendell, Daniel Burwell; First Baptist, Zebulon, Wm. Wright; Friendship Chapel, Sanders Dunn, H. Peppers, Chas. Heartfield, B. B. King, Hansel Dunn; Good Hope, Joseph Goodsin; Juniper Level, T. B. Smith, C. Bates, C. Morgan; Malaby's Cross Roads, B. W. Montague, F. Tate; Martin Street, W. A. Perry; Mt. Pleasant (Wake), A. Horton, Chas. Crudup, E. D. Hunter; New Liberty, L. H. Perry, Jr.; New Bethel, Thomas Morgan; Pleasant Grove, Frank Crews, F. M. Morgan; New Providence, W. L. Yates, J. Ray, H. Newkirk; Riley Hill, E. W. Mial, Lawrence Robertson; Union Grove, S. M. Mitchell, F. Harris; Wake Chapel, W. Price; Jones Hill, R. H. Jones; Gethsemane, H. B. Floyd.

COURSE OF STUDY FOR THOSE HAVING THE MINISTRY IN VIEW

Reading, writing, arithmetic, United States history, general history, geography, and Scripture geography, theology, systematic theology (Mullins), The Church (Harvey), Deaconship (Howell), Church Discipline (Hiscox), Homiletics (Broadus), History of the Baptist Denomination.

The course of study was adopted unanimously by the Association, and the churches are requested to license no person who cannot pass a creditable examination on reading, writing, the fundamental principles of arithmetic, grammar and geography, and to ordain no person who has not been before the Board of Examiners and recommended by them for ordination.

CONSTITUTION

Article I.   This body shall be known as the "Wake Baptist Association."

Art. II.   The object of this Association shall be the promotion of Christ's Kingdom among men, and the means of accomplishing this shall be in strict conformity with the New Testament.

Art. III.   This Association shall be composed of delegates chosen by the churches connected with it, each church being entitled to at least one delegate, and the one delegate for each hundred members or fraction thereof.   Ministers who are members of the churches connected with this body shall be considered members of the Association ex officio, and ministers who are not in charge or connected with churches within the bounds of this Association, who present testimonials of good standing in the Baptist denomination, may become members of this Association by payment of $1.00 annually.   **Provided,** ministers who aided in the organization of this Association shall be considered members so long as they are in good standing in the Baptist denomination; also any layman in good standing in the Baptist church may become an annual member by the payment of $1.00.

Art. IV.   The delegates from each church shall bear a letter certifying their appointment, giving an account of the condition of the church, and a statement of all funds contributed for benevolent purposes during the year.

Art. V.   The officers of this body shall be a Moderator, Vice-Moderator, Clerk, Corresponding Secretary, Treasurer, Auditor and a Statistician, whose duties shall be such as are generally performed by such officers.   In addition there shall be appointed a Home Mission Board, Foreign Mission Board, Educational Board, Sunday School Board, and an Executive Board, which latter shall have charge of the work of the Association during the interim of its annual session, and three members of the Executive Board shall constitute a quorum, and the officers of the body shall be ex officio members.   The other boards shall have supervision of the work of the Association along their several lines, subject to the Executive Board and the Association, and shall so organize the territory of the Association as to accomplish the best results, but not contrary to the Executive Board of the Association.

Art. VI. It shall be the duty of the Moderator to preside during the deliberations of the body, to enforce an observance of the Constitution, preserve the decorum, appoint committees, decide all questions of order, give his opinion concerning any subject under discussion after others have spoken or when called upon, and give the casting vote if a tie.

Art. VII. It shall be the duty of the clerk to report the proceedings of each annual session and superintend the printing and distribution of the minutes among the churches.

Art. VIII. It shall be the duty of the Treasurer to receive all funds sent up by the churches or collected during the session of this body, and disburse the same for the purpose for which they were sent or collected. He shall not pay any order on the Treasurer except it is signed by the Moderator and the Clerk of the Association subject to the provisions in the By-Laws.

Art. IX. Any church desiring to become a member of this body shall present her petition at an annual session of the Association through delegates appointed for that purpose, and if the Association shall consent to receive her the Moderator shall extend to the delegate the right hand of fellowship.

Art. X. This Association shall not maintain fellowship with any church that does not preserve Gospel order.

Art. XI. This Association may invite visiting brethren to seats and extend to them all privileges of the body save that of voting. The Association shall meet on Wednesday before the third Sabbath in August at such place as the Association may select.

Art. XII. All ministers composing the Association shall hold three ministerial meetings a year in such places as the brethren may designate.

Art. XIII. We will receive no ministers into this Association but those who have a good moral character.

Art. XIV. Any Baptist Sunday School or Missionary Society within the bounds of this Association may become a member of this Association, by sending voluntary contributions. Each shall be entitled to one delegate.

Art. XV. We will withdraw the right hand of fellowship from every minister who walks disorderly and contrary to the Gospel rule.

Art. XVI. Each church connected with this Association can continue its membership by supporting this Constitution.

Art. XVII. By appointment of the Association there shall be preached during each session an introductory sermon.

Art. XVIII. This Constitution may be amended at any annual session by a vote of two-thirds of the members present.

BY-LAWS

Section 1.   Schools, societies and individuals shall be acknowledged in the Minutes of the Association.

Sec. 2.   Before the final adjournment of the Association all the funds, notes, etc., shall be counted by the Finance Committee and Treasurer.   The Treasurer shall give the Finance Committee a receipt for the amount placed in his hands.

Sec. 3.   The Treasurer shall pay out no money except on order written by the Clerk and signed by the Moderator.

Sec. 4.   After the expenses of the Association shall have been paid the remaining Associational funds shall be applied to such purposes as the Association may direct.   The Executive Board shall execute plans adopted by the Association.

Sec. 5.   The Auditor shall audit the accounts of the Treasurer and make annual reports to the Association.

Sec. 6.   The duties of the Boards provided for in the Constitution shall be such as are usually performed by such boards in other similar bodies.

OUTLINE OF WORK

1. Call meeting to order.
2. Address of welcome.
3. Response.
4. Annual sermon.
5. Enrollment of messengers.
6. Appointment of committees.
7. Report of various boards.
    (a) Home Mission.
    (b) Foreign Mission.
    (c) Educational.
    (d) Sunday School.
    (e) Ministerial.
8. Report of Treasurer.
9. Report of Committees.
10. Miscellaneous Business.
11. Address
    (a) On Missions.
    (b) Educational Work.

LIST OF COMMITTEES

Enrollment—Revs. C. C. Jones, Prof. W. L. Price, Hoyt Mangum.

Place of Next Meeting—Revs. D. P. Lewis, N. A. Cheek, Bros. Jno. Lockley, J. W. Austin Knuckles, Chas. Young, J. H. Dednam, E. B. Thompson.

Temperance—Rev. Chas. A. Marriott, Dr. G. W. Moore, Bros. J. W. Crudup, W. H. Hawkins, Louis Brodie, Irving Pulley, Jas. A. Watkins.

Resolutions—Dr. O. S. Bullock, Revs. B. F. Jordan, P. H. Hedgepeth, Bros. J. H. Hayes, C. L. Perry, H. L. Clemons, and Robert Haskin.

Education—Profs. J. L. Levister, Berry O. Wilcox, Revs. Chas. H. Williamson, A. Evans, and E. L. Crudup.

Finance—Revs. C. C. Clark, W. C. Somerville, Bros. O. V. Carpenter, J. H. Cooke, Guyon Perry, W. T. Alston.

Moderator's Address—Dr. G. W. Moore, Revs. C. C. Jones, N. A. Cheek, Bros. J. H. Ellis, C. W. Laws, and Prof. J. L. Levister.

Hours of Meeting—Revs. P. H. Hedgepeth, W. C. Somerville, E. D. Murray, J. A. Hawkins, Rufus Jones, A. L. Cooke, R. B. Mangum, Irving Pulley, R. B. Raeford.

Obituary—Revs. H. D. Eaton, Wm. Smith, T. J. Foster, Bros. S. H. High, J. D. Taylor, B. J. Faison, E. D. Murray, Joseph Ray.

On Publication of Miss Bass' Paper—Rev. W. C. Somerville, H. D. Eaton, and J. L. Levister.

MODERATOR'S RECOMMENDATIONS

1. That each church of the Association have a Bible School of at least one week's length, presided over by such persons as the church may appoint, at the expense of the church.

2. That a Training Class be established for the instruction of church officers, to meet twice per year, to drill them in church duties, at the cost of those churches who institute the work.

3. That the standard be $.60 per member per year for Missions and Christian Education.

4. That we endorse and support the President of Shaw, Dr. Wm. Stuart Nelson, in the work of the school.

5. That each minister pay one dollar per year for the support of our older ministers.

6. That the Teacher Training Course be adopted and put in vogue in our churches.

PROCEEDINGS

The Sixty-Sixth Annual Session of the Wake Baptist Association met with the Felts Chapel Baptist Church, near Youngsville, N. C., August 17, 1932, at 10:00 o'clock a.m., with Rev. M. W. Williams, Moderator, presiding.

An impressive praise service was conducted by Rev. A. A. Morrissey and Bro. Robert Jones. Brother Jones read a part of the 13th chapter of I. Cor. following the singing of song No. 674 in the Baptist Hymn Book, lined by Rev. Morrissey. Then Brother Morrissey offered prayer.

The church pastor, Rev. P. H. Hedgepeth, was presented by the Moderator to give the Welcome Address to the delegates.

Dr. Geo. W. Moore, of Raleigh, gave the response in fitting words.

Following the naming of the Committee on Enrollment (See Com.), echoes from the field were heard from the following brethren representing their church: O. V. Carpenter, Friendship Chapel; B. Morgan, New Bethel; R. Haskin, First Baptist, Wilson; A. J. Hawkins, New Liberty; H. Cook, Felts Chapel; J. A. Perry, Riley Hill; J. D. Fryson, Mt. Zion, Raleigh; C. L. Perry, Jones Hill; E. W. Crudup, First Baptist, Raleigh; A. Hawkins, South Main St., Louisburg; C. Y. King, Baptist Grove, J. H. Cook, First Baptist, Franklinton; Prof. H. Price, Martin Street, Raleigh; H. R. Snow, Springfield; D. Nicholson, Gethsemane; O. L. Bridges, Elevation; and Sister Allen, of White Oak. All reports gave testimony of some progress in Kingdom advancement through the church herein named.

Rev. B. F. Jordan, pastor First Baptist Church, Wilson, N. C., then ascended the rostrum to preach the Annual Sermon, accompanied by Dr. O. S. Bullock and Rev. D. P. Lewis.

The theme of Brother Jordan's message was, "God, the Refuge of His People," based on Psalms 46:1.

Subsequent the able message, song, "Amazing Grace" was sung by the congregation.

The Committees on Hours of Meeting and Finance, respectively, were appointed. (See Committee.)

An offering of $6.05 was taken by Dr. J. B. Davis and Rev. Wm. Smith.

The report of the Committee on Hours of Meeting was then made. (See report.) Adopted.

The following visitors were then introduced to the House: Rev. Murphy, pastor First Baptist Church, Louisburg; Mrs. Geo. S. Stokes, Mrs. M. W. Williams, and Mrs. James Clark, of State Normal School, Elizabeth City, N. C.

Benediction by Rev. N. A. Cheek.

WEDNESDAY AFTERNOON SESSION

Following an inspirational song service conducted by Rev. W. A. Perry and C. D. Jones, echoes from the field were continued and the following named persons appeared for their church: S. H. High, Wakefield; B. Hinton, Good Hope; Joseph Ray, New Providence; G. Gill, Wake Chapel; R. B. Mangum, Woodland Chapel; Rev. A. Horton, Mt. Pleasant (Wake); J. W. Crudup, Gethsemane; Irving Pulley, White Oak; Rev. W. C. Somerville, pastor, Wakefield; and Rev. C. D. Jones, St. Matthews.

"I Am Dwelling In Beulah Land," was sung, led by Rev. P. H. Hedgepeth, following which the Moderator gave his annual message while Rev. B. F. Jordan, Vice-Moderator, presided. "What Hath God Wrought" was the theme of the message. Comprehensive and practical was the message of the Moderator.

Subsequent some favorable comment on the message by Drs. O. S. Bullock and G. W. Moore, of Raleigh, a Committee on Moderator's Address was named. (See Committee.)

"Church Ordinances, Their Significance and Importance" was discussed in an able way by Rev. W. C. Somerville. Rev. H. D. Eaton, Dr. G. W. Moore and Rev. C. F. Pope made some remarks on the subject.

Motion prevailed that the topic, "The Relation of Baptist Organizations," be discussed Thursday a.m. at 10:30 o'clock.

After some announcements, Rev. P. H. Hedgepeth pronounced the benediction.

WEDNESDAY EVENING SESSION

Beginning at 7:30 o'clock an interesting program of one hour length, was rendered by the Woman's Auxiliary of the Association. Long live the Auxiliary.

Rev. T. J. Foster then conducted a short praise service, read for a lesson a part of II Tim. 1 chapter; following which, Bro. Luke Jones offered prayer.

Rev. J. H. Clanton was presented to preach the Doctrinal Sermon, by Rev. W. C. Somerville, the presiding officer for the evening. The text of the message was found II Tim. 1:12.

The message of the speaker was effectively delivered to a large audience.

Mrs. Finch sang "There Is a Happy Land Beyond," and an offering of $2.25 was taken.

Mrs. J. H. Clanton was introduced to the audience and made some remarks.

Benediction by Rev. J. H. Clanton.

THURSDAY MORNING SESSION

Beginning at 10:00 o'clock Bros. E. L. Crudup and T. B. Smith conducted an impressive song service. Thirteen verses of Matt. 5th chapter were read by Brother Smith, and Brother Luke Jones offered prayer.

Brothers Chas. Young, of Wake Chapel; and Smith, of Elevation, spoke in the interest of their churches to the body.

"What Youth Expects of the Church" was ably discussed by Miss Ann Bass, a recent graduate of Shaw University. Among other things Miss Bass stressed (1) "Adequate instruction, (2) Activity and service, and (3) Opportunity to participate in its rights and activities."

Rev. W. C. Somerville also set forth, on the subject, among other things, (1) "Education, (2) Self-Expression, (3) The proper example."

On motion made by Rev. C. H. Williamson the paper outlined by Miss Bass was voted to go into the minutes.

Our Relation to Baptist Organizations (a) The minister's was discussed by Rev. C. C. Jones. (b) "The minister of the church should know of the workings of the State Convention and present himself at each meeting and work for the cause," averred the speaker.

The message was timely and ably delivered.

A Committee on Publication was named.   (See Committee.)

The Deacon's Relations were set forth by Dr. Geo. W. Moore. "The deacon should open the service when the pastor is absent," declared Dr. Moore.

After singing "More Like Jesus," Rev. D. P. Lewis spoke on the general church member's relation. "The member should follow the leader, study the church program, the Association and general Convention."

"Support the church financially and spiritually." The message was strong and thoughtful.

"Everybody Will Be Happy Over There," was sung by Mrs. Finch.

Mrs. Cora Pair Thomas, returned missionary from Africa, then came to the floor and made a strong appeal for the work of Missions, relating some of her experiences on the Mission Field.

Three classes of people were named by Mrs. Thomas, (1) Those who are partly trained by attending schools, such as are there (2) Those who are desirous to become Christians, and (3) Those who know nothing about God.

"Take the Name of Jesus With You" was sung, then the report of the Foreign Mission Board was made by Rev. D. P. Lewis, and an offering taken for Missions amounting to $9.47.

Rev. D. P. Lewis, Rev. W. C. Somerville, and Rev. M. W. Williams, each paid $1.00 in the offering. Rev. P. H. Hedgepeth, 50c; Rev. Wm. Smith, 25c, while many others gave smaller sums of money.

Benediction by Rev. C. D. Jones.

THUSRDAY AFTERNOON SESSION

Dr. Geo. W. Moore conducted a touching song service and Rev. Chas. A. Marriott read the 24th Psalm as a scripture lesson, then offered prayer.

The Treasurer, Rev. C. C. Clark, made his report. (See report.) Adopted.

A report on Education was given. (See report.) Adopted.

The following named committees then made their reports: Officers, Temperance, Place of Next Meetng. (See reports.)

The report of the Committee on Place recommended "Olive Branch" Church, Wake Forest, N. C., as the next meeting place of the Annual Session. A letter was presented to the House from Mt. Bright Church, Hillsboro, N. C., asking for the session. Then a standing vote was taken on the two named places. For Hillsboro, the number was 25. For "Olive Branch," 31. Olive Branch was declared as the place of next meeting.

The report of Committee on Obituary was made, and with bowed heads, standing, the congregation sang, "Only Remembered By What We Have Done."

The Committee on Resolutions made its report. (See report). Adopted with an amendment that churches holding only one regular service per month be urged to have two regular services.

Dean J. L. Tilley, of Shaw University, then was presented to speak. The message was mainly based on the saying, "I send you forth as lambs among wolves." "I want you to be wisely good and goodly wise," averred the speaker. Among other things some fundamentals were laid down as a basis to develop Christian character. (1) The Home, (2) Sunday School, (3.) A strong institution to train youth.

The message was powerfully delivered and joyfully received by all present.

"A Charge to Keep I Have," was sung by the congregation.

The Woman's Auxiliary made its report of $44.00 and many garments for the Mission Field. "Many young people have come into the Auxiliary," declared Mrs. N. A. Hunter.

The report was adopted with many thanks to the faithful women.

The Committee on Finance made its report and the Committee on Moderator's Address. (See reports.) Adopted.

A closing song, "Till We Meet at Jesus' Feet," was sung and Rev. P. H. Hedgepeth pronounced the benediction.

THE EXTRA SESSION

The Extra Session of the Wake Baptist Association met with the Tupper Memorial Baptist Church, Raleigh, N. C., Sunday, March 20, 1932, at 10:30 a.m.

Moderator Williams called the House to order and Bros. C. A. Marriott and C. C. Jones conducted devotionals with the church choir rendering music.

Following some congratulatory remarks by the Moderator and thanking God for His care and keeping power, Mrs. B. E. Barrett, President of the Woman's Auxiliary, urged the delegations to give more liberally to Missions and thus enrich the Kingdom of God.

Mrs. M. N. Perry declared, the purpose of the Auxiliary is "to make soldiers for Christ."

Miss Susie Wilcox stressed the importance of a Christian background in the Lord's work, and when this is done there will be liberality in the Lord's work.

"The Church in Social Adjustments" was discussed by Rev. V. T. Williams. In part the speaker said, "The church is the light and it must carry the light of intelligence, truth, love, good-will, Christian tolerance and purity."

Rev. C. C. Jones, on the subject, declared that "Christ commissioned the church to save souls, and this is the only institution so delegated with power."

Dean John L. Tilley, of Shaw University, was then presented to preach, who complimented the Association on its work done for Missions and Christian Education and chose for a theme, "The Place and Task of the Church in the World Today." The message grew out of Matt. 28:19-20 as a text, "Go ye," etc. Among other things the speaker

PROGRAM

OF THE

SIXTY SEVENTH ANNUAL SESSION

OF THE

WAKE BAPTIST ASSOCIATION

AND THE

FIFTEENTH ANNUAL SESSION

OF THE

WOMAN'S AUXILIARY

TO BE HELD WITH

THE OLIVE BRANCH BAPTIST CHURCH

REV. H. Y. CHEEK, PASTOR

WAKE FORSET, NORTH CAROLINA

AUGUST 16-17, 1933

WEDNESDAY MORNING SESSION

10:00-Devotionals-Rev.O.C.Jones,Rev.M.M.Smit
10:10-Address of Welcome-Rev.H.Y.Cheek-Pasto
10:30-Response-Rev.A.E.Johnson.
10:40-Echoes from the Field.
11:00-Enrollment Messengers-Naming Committe
11:10-How to Finance the Church-Dr.O.S.Bull
11:50-Annual Sermon-Rev.C.A.Marriott.
12:00-Offering--Adjournment.

WEDNESDAY AFTERNOON SESSION

2:00-Spirituals-Rev.J.H.Hedgpeth,Rev.J.H.Co
2:10-Echoes from the Field.
2:20-Moderation Address-Rev.M.W.Williams.
2:40-The Lord's Supper:
  (a).How Administered, Rev.D.P.Lewis.
  (b) The Participants, Rev.V.T.Williams.
      (20 minutes each speaker)
3:20-Church Discipline,Rev.C.F.Pope,
     Rev.N.A.Cheek.
      (15 minutes each speaker)
3:50-Report of Committees.
4:10-Introduction of Visitors.
4:20-Offering----Adjournment.

WEDNESDAY EVENING SESSION

7:30-Program of the Woman's Auxiliary.
8:30-Spirituals-Rev.D.H.Holt,Rev.C.Evans.
8:35-Sermon--Rev. H.D.Eaton.
9:20-Offering---Adjournment.

THURSDAY MORNING SESSION

10:00-Devotionals-Rev.W.T.Farror,Rev.W.L.W
10:10-Echoes from the Field.
10:25-What the Church Expects of Youth,
      Rev.A.A.Morrissey, Rev.C.C.Clark.
11:00-The Wake Association's Part in a Grea
      Shaw University,President W.S.Nelson

11:40-Address-Dr. J.P.Gulla, Dean of the
      School of Religion, Wake Forest
      College.
12:10-Offering.
12:20-Introduction of Visitors.
12:30-Adjournment.
       THURSDAY AFTERNOON SESSION
2:30-Devotionals-Rev.W.H.Rogers,
      Rev. J.R.Dent.
2:40-North Carolina Baptist's Program,
      Dr.C.S.Brown, General Secretary.
3:20-Report of Committees.
3:40-Introduction of Visitors.
3:50-Announcements.
4:40-Benediction.
     WOMAN'S AUXILIARY PROGRAM
     TUESDAY NIGHT SESSION
7:30-Praise service-Sisters Annie Freeman
      and N.A.Hunter.
7:40-Welcome Address-Rev.H.Y.Cheek-Pastor
8:00-Response-Miss Sussie Wilcox.
8:15-Annual Sermon-Rev.V.T.Williams.
9:00-Offering.
9:15-Introduction of Visitors-
      Announcements.
9:30-Adjournment.
     WEDNESDAY MORNING SESSION
10:00-Praise service-Sisters Emma Smith
      and Viola Riddick.
10:10-Enrollment of Delegates-Naming
      Committees.
10:20-Echoes from the Field.
10:45-Why does Christ Need Young People?
      Miss Lena Marriott, Mrs.L.Foster.
11:30-Offering.

11:45-Introduction of Visitors.
12:00-Adjournment.
WEDNESDAY AFTERNOON SESSION
2:00-Praise service-Sisters Essie Bake,
    and Carolina Rayford.
2:10-Quartet selection, led by
    Mitchel Hunter.
2:20-President's Annual Message.--
    Mrs. B.E.Barrett.
2:55-Paper--Mrs. A.A.Morrissey.
3:10-Remarks--Rev. J.F.Haywood.
3:25-Solo-Miss Howell
#:35-Offering--Adjournment.
WEDNESDAY EVENING SESSION
7z30-Program by Local Auxiliary.
THURSDAY MORNING SESSION
10:00-Devotionals-Mrs. Mary Marable.
    Mrs. Cora Leach.
10:25-The Personality of Jesus, It's
    Helpfulness to Youth-Mrs.W.C.Sommerv
10:45-Some of the World's greatest Needs. t
    day, and How Youth may supply them--
    Mrs. J.H.Clanton.
11:45-How may Adults better Understand You
    People? Mrs.M. W.Williams.
11:45-Team work in the Church among Adults
    and Young People--Mrs. G.S.Stokes.
12:15-Report of Committees.
12:25 Offering.
12:30-Benediction.

said, "That Jesus is concerned with making a better society." "Christians are to make Jesus re-live in the world."

The message was uplifting and helpful to those who heard it, profound in thought and spiritual in force.

An offering of $5.00 was taken after the message.

AFTERNOON SESSION

A delicious dinner was served at Shaw University dining hall and the exercises began in the University Chapel at 2:30 o'clock with singing "Let My People Go," by the Shaw Quartette.

President Nelson was then presented and welcomed the organization to Shaw in able words. In part, Dr. Nelson declared, "The church must plant the right principles in youth before the March winds of temptation turn them about." "Church motives are unselfish, not selfish."

Thanks were extended the brethren for what they had done to help Shaw carry on.

"Steal Away" was sung by the choir.

The report of Committee on Resolutions was read by Miss Phillis Stancil. (See report.) Adopted by standing.

An offering of $81.21 was taken by Dr. O. S. Bullock and Brother Blunt, of Louisburg, for Shaw.

Faculty members who paid in the rally, and the amount: Professor Harris, $1.00; Professor Price, $1.00; Mrs. Redfern, $2.00; Professor Perrin, $3.00; President Nelson, $5.00; Dean Tilley, $5.00; Miss Shamberger, $5.00; Professor Coker, $10.00; Miss Martin, $10.00; and Dr. Redfern, $15.00.

Some others who gave: Rev. O. S. Bullock, $1.00; Brother Blunt, $1.00; Brother Johnson, $1.00; Brother M. D. Haywood, $1.00; Rev. G. S. Stokes, $1.00; Rev. M. W. Williams, $13.50.

President Nelson then introduced the following members of the faculty: Dean John L. Tilley, Prof. H. C. Perrin, Prof. N. H. Harris, Dr. F. C. Redfern, Prof. C. R. Eason, Mrs. V. K. Cameron, Miss B. E. Parham, Prof. Joseph H. Wortham, Miss E. Shamberger, Prof. Geo. C. Coker, Miss

A. Ruth Gadson, Prof. Harry Gil-Smythe, Prof. W. B. Turner, and Prof. J. F. Price. Dean Tilley spoke for the group in fitting remarks.

The Finance Committee then made its report. (See report.) Adopted.

On behalf of the school, President Nelson thanked the Association for its presence and gift.

The benediction was pronounced by Rev. M. L. Dawson.

THE MINISTERIAL UNION

The Wake Ministers' and Deacons' Union is an important part of the Association, holding its meeting each fifth Saturday and Sunday in the bounds of the Association.

The Union is purposed to be a schooling for all Christians and especially ministers and deacons, in the doctrine and practices of the Baptist church growing out of the New Testament scripture.

Charity, Missions and Christian Education are the supported objects of the Union at each meeting.

FOREIGN MISSION BOARD REPORT

The words of our Lord, "Provide neither gold nor silver nor brass in your purses. Neither scrip for your journey, neither two coats, neither shoes"; pretty well describe the condition of a large proportion of our foreign missionaries. Many of them after going to their mission fields and seeing the great needs facing them from day to day have not only given their all but lives. Certainly no more self-sacrificing group than our foreign missionaries can be found anywhere in our denomination.

Mrs. Cora Pair Thomas is in the State now urging the Baptists to rally to the support of our mission station in Liberia.

In view of the many urgent and pathetic appeals for help from all of the foreign fields and especially from Africa: We recommend the following:

1. That the Association record its feeling that the preaching of the Gospel to all the world should be the primary emphasis of the church and that this be kept constantly in mind, especially during these days when decreasing appropriations are necessitating the radical curtailment of the Foreign Mission work.

2. That churches, societies, and individuals assume, wherever possible definite responsibility for definite parts of the Foreign Mission work.

3. That ministers and other church leaders be encouraged to use their facilities and influence, in impressing Foreign Mission work upon their people.

4. That all Sunday Schools be urged this year to assume some part of the Foreign Mission work as their specific responsibility.

D. P. LEWIS,
Chairman.

REPORT ON EDUCATION

We, your Committee on Education, wish to submit the following: We recommend and encourage the untiring interest in the general education of our people, and urge them to avail themselves of all opportunities for keeping their children in the schools during the school sessions.

We further reaffirm our pledge to support Shaw University and congratulate President Nelson for his year of successful management of Shaw. And urge the churches of this Association to formulate a systematic plan for contributing to Shaw.

Respectfully submitted,

COMMITTEE.

REPORT OF COMMITTEE ON OBITUARY

We, your Committee on Obituary, beg to submit the following:

Whereas, it has pleased Almighty God to call unto Himself many faithful members of the various churches of this Association whose labors and presence we miss, Be it resolved:

That we pause for a short time and pay due respect to their memory in suitable service. Among many we mention, Rev. J. C. Love.

Respectfully,

COMMITTEE.

RESOLUTIONS

In view of the fact that we are in the midst of one of the greatest economic depressions known in mordern history and that it has a tendency to affect the Christian church attendance and support. Be it resolved:

1. That this Association go on record as urging its constituency to give more loyal support to the churches throughout its bounds.

2. That we urge our pastors to give a very thorough study of the scripture so that they may give a true' interpretation to God's Word in the light of the modern day and condition.

3. Since Shaw University has made such rapid progress under the leadership of Dr. Wm. Stuart Nelson with so much of its resources discontinued, be it resolved that the Wake Association ask its churches to support more loyally the University in their mid-year Association and their two special Shaw days.

4. That this body express its deep appreciation and thanks to the pastor, members, and friends of Felts Chapel Baptist Church for their loyal and gracious support of this Association.

5. That churches be urged to use two Sundays per month for service.

Respectfully,

COMMITTEE.

TEMPERANCE COMMITTEE REPORT

Whereas, America is increasing in crime and other evils, which are caused by intemperance; We therefore, recommend;

1. That pastors, deacons, superintendents, and teachers practice and teach temperance in all things.

2. That parents teach their children against the dance hall, keeping late hours at night and excessive automobile riding.

3. That pastors and school teachers inform the youth of the awful harm in violating the prohibition law.

4. That the churches in this body refuse calling a man as pastor who indulges in the drink and other immoral habits.

5. That pastors, teachers, and superintendents work together cooperatively and whole-heartedly in their respective communities for the enforcement of the Eighteenth Amendment.

Respectfully submitted,

THE COMMITTEE.

REPORT ON PLACE OF NEXT MEETING

We, your Committee, recommend Olive Branch Baptist Church, Wake Forest, N. C., as the next Annual Meeting place.

COMMITTEE.

REPORT ON HOURS OF MEETING

Adjourn at 1:30 p.m., re-assemble, 2:30; close at pleasure.

For Thursday Session—

Open at 10 o'clock a.m.; dinner 1:30 p.m.; re-assemble at 2:30 p.m., and close at pleasure.

COMMITTEE.

REPORT ON RESOLUTIONS

In view of the fact that the Wake Baptist Association endorses and supports Christian Education through its financial support of Shaw University, be it resolved· .

1. That the Association redouble its efforts to organize its forces so that every member will be reached in making his contribution to Christian Education through Shaw University,

2. That we endorse strongly the administration of President Nelson and give our continued support in a moral as well as a financial way in Wake County and the State as well.

3. That we endorse strongly the wonderful sermon given by Dean Tilley, of Shaw University, in which he stated clearly and impulsively the principles of Christian Education to be carried throughout the State of North Carolina; and the mission of the church in cooperating with the schools and preparing teachers to develop Christian personalities in the school.

Respectfully submitted,

REV. C. C. JONES,

Chairman;

REV. J. F. HAYWOOD,

REV. G. O. WATKINS,

REV. O. S. BULLOCK,

PROFESSOR J. L. LEVISTER,

MR. T. W. HARRIS,

MR. J. S. JONES,

MISS PHYLLIS A. STANCIL,

Secretary.

REPORT OF COMMITTEE ON OFFICERS

We recommend the following named persons for officers of this body for the ensuing year: Revs. M. W. Williams, Moderator; B. F. Jordan, Vice-Moderator; Geo. S. Stokes, Clerk; A. A. Morrissey, Corresponding Secretary; C. C. Clark, Treasurer; Chas. A. Marriott, Auditor; and   , Statistician.

Respectfully,

COMMITTEE.

REPORT OF TREASURER

FROM AUGUST 12, 1931, TO AUGUST 17, 1932

Money raised...$ 787.57

Disbursements:

Lott Carey Convention.....................................	100.00
Mrs. B. E. Barrett (traveling expenses)..........	12.00
J. L. Levister (transfer expenses)	2.00
Shaw University	300.00
Mrs. L. B. Foster (Asso. expenses)	1.60
M. W. Williams (provisions for Founders' Day)	18.00
Mrs. N. A. Hunter (Asso. expenses)	1.00
Shaw University (groceries)	5.40
Geo. S. Stokes (mailing letters)	3.00
Capital Printing Company (Union Reformer)..	40.00
Shaw University	18.00
General Baptist Convention	50.00
Treasurer's expenses	3.75
For printing 300 programs	2.50
Mrs. C. Hall (service)	1.50
Mrs. J. C. Love (charity)	1.35
Rev. A. G. Seawell (charity)	10.00
Union Reformer (donation)	25.00
Rev. Geo. S. Stokes (service)	50.00
Bynum Printing Co.	43.00
Delegate General Convention expenses	6.00
General Baptist Convention Representation fee	50.00
Rev. M. L. Dawson (charity)	2.00
Rev. M. W. Williams (expense)	5.00
Rev. A. A. Morrissey (stamps, paper).............	3.00
Capital Printing Co. (on Baptist Debt)	50.00
Reformer (donation)	25.00
Treasurer's expenses	6.00

Money collected ....$ 787.57
Money brought forward 81.30
Money paid out 835.10
Money on hand 33.77

C. C. CLARK,
Treasurer.

I find the report of the Treasurer to be correct.

CHARLES A. MARRIOTT,
Auditor.

FINANCE COMMITTEE REPORT

We, your Committee on Finance, do hereby submit the following report:

	Commencement	Extra Session S. S.	Extra Session	Annual Session
Baptist Grove	$	$	$ 12.00	$ 10.00
Bethlehem	....	......	....	8.00
Dawson Street, Raleigh	....	......	....	....
Elevation	....	......	....	4.00
Elizabeth	....	......	....	1.20
Felts Chapel	....	......	....	6.00
First Baptist, Bailey	....	......	....	....
First Baptist, Franklinton	6.75	......	....	5.67
Franklin County B. Y. P. U.	15.00	......	....	....
First Baptist, Fuquay Springs	....	......	....	4.40
First Baptist, Raleigh	....	......	....	10.00
First Baptist, Wendell	.60	......	....	....
First Baptist, Wilson	....	......	....	....
First Baptist, Zebulon	.50	......	....	2.00
Friendship Chapel	1.00	......	....	6.05
Gethsemane	....	......	10.00	10.00
Good Hope	....	1.00	10.00	4.00
Holly Springs	....	......	....	....
Jones' Chapel	....	......	....	3.50
Jones Hill	....	......	....	3.00
Juniper Level	....	1.50	3.80	7.50
Macedonia	....	......	....	....
Malaby's Cross Roads	....	......	....	....
Mary Grove	....	......	....	13.00
Martin Street, Raleigh	....	......	25.00	25.00
Mt. Bright	....	......	....	7.00
Mt. Pleasant (Wake)	....	1.00	7.25	20.00
Mt. Pleasant (Franklin)	....	......	....	....
Mt. Zion (Cary)	....	......	.50	1.50
Mt. Zion (Raleigh)	....	......	....	2.00
New Bethel	....	......	....	6.05
New Hope	....	......	....	10.00
New Liberty	....	......	2.00	5.40
New Light	....	......	....	1.00
New Providence	....	......	....	10.00
Oak City Baptist	....	2.50	5.00	5.00
Oberlin Baptist	....	......	10.00	7.00
Olive Branch	....	......	....	2.50

FINANCE COMMITTEE REPORT—Continued

	Commence-ment	Extra Session S. S.	Extra Session
Open Field ....$	....	$ .78	$..........
Pilot Baptist	....	......	....
Pleasant Grove	....	......	....
River Dell	1.00	......	....
Riley Hill	2.00	1.65	20.00
Springfield	....	1.00	13.55
South Main Street, Louisburg......	....	......	21.00
Stokes Chapel	.50	......	3.00
St. Matthews	6.50	......	5.00
Tupper Memorial	....	......	8.75
Union Grove	....	......	....
Wake Chapel	....	1.00	....
Wakefield	5.00	......	7.75
Wake Baptist Grove	....	......	....
White Oak	.50	......	....
Williams Grove	....	......	2.00
Woodland Chapel	....	......	5.00
Public Collection	....	......	....
Woman's Auxiliary	....	......	....
Rev. M. W. Williams	10.00	......	....
Rev. W. C. Somerville	5.00	......	....
Wake Missionary Union	....	......	....
Wake Minister's Union	5.00	......	....
Rev. W. H. Rogers	1.00	......	....
Rev. W. M. Smith	1.00	......	....
Rev. Geo. S. Stokes	1.00	......	....

Respectfully submitted,

COMMI

The amount of money that each church is asked to raise d associational year for Missions and Christian Education, the State Baptist Convention:

Bethlehem ....$
Baptist Grove ....
Dawson Street, Raleigh ....
Elevation ....
Elizabeth ....
Felts Chapel ....
First Baptist, Bailey ....
First Baptist, Franklinton ....

First Baptist, Fuquay Springs ....$	25.00
First Baptist, Raleigh	200.00
First Baptist, Wendell	16.00
First Baptist, Wilson	100.00
First Baptist, Zebulon	15.00
Friendship Chapel	25.00
Gethsemane	25.00
Good Hope	50.00
Holly Springs	40.00
Jones Chapel	15.00
Jones Hill	50.00
Juniper Level	60.00
Macedonia	10.00
Malaby's Cross Roads	50.00
Mary's Grove	10.00
Martin Street, Raleigh	50.00
Mt. Bright, Hillsboro	26.00
Mt. Moriah	20.00
Mt. Pleasant (Wake)	50.00
Mt. Pleasant (Franklin)	10.00
Mt. Zion (Cary)	10.00
Mt. Zion (Raleigh)	10.00
New Bethel	58.00
New Hope	15.00
New Liberty	50.00
New Light	16.00
New Providence	48.00
Oak City Baptist	25.00
Oberlin Baptist	42.00
Olive Branch	50.00
Pilot Baptist	5.00
Pleasant Grove	52.00
River Dell	5.00
Riley Hill	100.00
Springfield	50.00
South Main Street, Louisburg	50.00
Stokes Chapel	25.00
St. Matthews	30.00
Tupper Memorial	50.00
Union Grove	40.00
Wake Chapel	25.00
Wakefield	50.00
White Oak	10.00
Woodland Chapel	25.00
Williams Grove	5.00
Wake Baptist Grove	30.00

Churches, Pastors, Postoffice	Preaching Sunday
Baptist Grove, V. T. Williams, Raleigh	3
Bethlehem, W. T. Farror, Franklinton	1
Dawson Street, J. F. Haywood, Raleigh	Ev. Sun.
Elevation, A. G. Seawell, Raleigh	1
Elizabeth, J. W. Evans	1
Felt's Chapel, P. H. Hedgepeth, Castalia	2
First Baptist, Bailey, F. Harrison, Nashville	2
First Baptist, Franklinton, M. W. Williams, Raleigh	2 and 4
First Baptist, Fuquay Springs, L. E. Johnson, Garner	3
First Baptist, Raleigh, O. S. Bullock, Raleigh	Ev. Sun.
First Baptist, Wendell, R. Crocket, Clayton	3
First Baptist, Wilson, B. F. Jordan, Wilson	Ev. Sun.
First Baptist, Zebulon, Chas. A. Marriott, Wendell	1
Friendship Chapel	1
Gethsemane, J. H. Jones, Durham	1
Good Hope, J. H. Clanton, Raleigh	2
Holly Springs	4
Jones Chapel, J. A. Jones, Knightdale	1
Jones Hill, A. A. Morrissey, Raleigh	2
Juniper Level, H. D. Eaton, Creedmoor	1
Macedonia, W. L. Wilson, Louisburg	3
Malaby's Cross Roads, R. Crocket, Clayton	4
Mary's Grove, W. F. Wilson, Louisburg	3
Martin Street, Raleigh, V. T. Williams	Ev. Sun.
Mt. Bright, A. B. Johnson, Raleigh	1 and 3
Mt. Pleasant (Wake), C. C. Clark, Raleigh	2 and 4
Mt. Pleasant (Franklin)	
Mt. Zion, Cary, Wm. Smith, State College Station, Raleigh	4
Mt. Zion, Raleigh, Wm. A. Perry, Raleigh	Ev. Sun.
New Bethel, J. W. Powell, Wake Forest	4
New Hope, A. A. Hartley, Clayton	1
New Liberty, N. A. Cheek, Elberon	1
New Light, J. W. Powell, Wake Forest	2
New Providence	2
Oak City, Geo. S. Stokes, Middlesex	2 and 4
Oberlin Baptist, A. A. Morrissey, Raleigh	Ev. Sun.
Olive Branch, H. Y. Cheek, Henderson	1 and 3
Pilot Baptist, P. H. Hedgepeth, Castalia	4
Pleasant Grove, H. Haskin, Oxford	4
River Dell	1
Riley Hill, Geo. S. Stokes, Middlesex	2
Springfield, M. W. Williams, Raleigh	1 and 3
South Main Street, Louisburg, D. P. Lewis, Louisburg	Ev. Sun.
Stokes Chapel	4
St. Matthew's, Wm. Smith, Raleigh	3

Churches, Pastors, Postoffice   *Preaching Sunday*

Tupper Memorial, C. C. Jones, Raleigh..Ev. Sun.

Union Grove, L. A. Brooks, Kittrell... 2

Wake Baptist Grove, J. W. Powell, Wake Forest............................ 3

Wake Chapel, J. W. Jones, Wilsons Mills.. 4

Wakefield, W. C. Somerville, Raleigh......:.. 3

White Oak, W. M. Moore, Enfield... 3

Williams Grove, Wm. Smith, Raleigh... 1

Woodland Chapel, Eli Thompson, Durham...................................... 4

STATISTICS OF ASSOCIATIONAL YEAR

Number of members added by baptism and letter.......................... 684

Number of members lost by death and exclusion............................. 270

Net gain... 414

Value of church property..$200,000

Name of Church and Clerk	Membership		
	Male	Female	Total
Baptist Grove, I. L. Leathers, Raleigh, R. 6	73	130	203
Bethlehem, Miss Lillie Canady, Raleigh, R. 6	75	125	200
Dawson Street, Raleigh	......	......	......
Elevation, John Seawell, Raleigh	29	14	53
Elizabeth, N. W. Pulley, Spring Hope, R. 1, Box 220	43	71	114
Felts Chapel, Rufus Jones, Louisburg, R. 1	41	71	112
First Baptist, Bailey, J. L. Ricks, Bailey, R. 1	40	45	85
First Baptist, Franklinton, Mrs. Mattie Smith, Box 287	198	254	452
First Baptist, Fuquay Springs, W. G. Allen, R. 1, Box 20	90	110	200
First Baptist, Raleigh, Dr. Geo. T. Jones, E. Cabarrus St.	251	704	955
First Baptist, Wendell, Mrs. Lula Rogers, Wendell	35	70	105.
First Baptist, Wilson	......	......	......
First Baptist, Zebulon, H. D. Wright, Zebulon, R. 1	26	42	68
Friendship Chapel, Geo. Kittrell, Wake Forest, R. 3	53	123	176
Gethsemane, J. W. Crudup, Louisburg	115	154	269
Good Hope, A. I. Goodson, Raleigh, R. 2	35	65	100
Holly Springs, J. R. Burt, Holly Springs	65	61	126
Jones Chapel, W. A. Jones, Knightdale, R. —, Box 22	28	30	58
Jones Hill, S. B. Dunn, Zebulon, R. 2	91	125	216
Juniper Level, W. R. Smith, McCullers, R. 1	108	115	223
Macedonia	23	20	43
Malaby's Cross Roads, Miss E. G. Smith, Raleigh, R. 5, Box 35	77	155	232
Mary Grove	......	......	60
Martin Street, Raleigh	......	......	310
Mt. Bright, G. C. Faribault, Hillsboro	40	76	137
Mt. Pleasant (Wake), O. A. Allen	......	......	260
Mt. Zion (Cary), J. W. Turner, Cary	6	24	30
Mt. Zion (Raleigh), P. G. Wells, Jr.	5	9	14
New Bethel, F. D. Fowler, Wake Forest, R. 2	131	202	333
New Hope, Mrs. Susie Williams, Spring Hope	6	23	29
New Liberty, Isaac Cook, Louisburg, R. F. D.	90	110	200
New Light, Otis Garrett, Creedmoor, R. 1	24	29	53
New Providence, W. N. Utley, Varina, R. 1	121	150	271
Oak City, Berry Wilcox, Method	60	75	135
Oberlin Baptist	69	148	217
Olive Branch, Mrs. Ellen T. Powell, Wake Forest	60	122	182
Pilot Baptist, Mrs. J. W. Thomas, Spring Hope, R. 1	23	27	50
Pleasant Grove, J. H. Debnam, Wendell	87	110	197
River Dell, S. M. McCullers, Wendell, R. 1	5	4	9
Riley Hill, Guyon Perry, Wendell, R. 2	208	317	525
Springfield, T. J. Seawell, Raleigh, R. 2	125	185	310
South Main Street, Louisburg, Mrs. Martha Leonard	112	248	360
Stokes Chapel, W. M. Todd, Middlesex	40	60	100

Name of Church and Clerk	Membership Male	Female	Tot
St. Matthews, Moses Hunter, Raleigh, R. 5..............................	75	150	2!
Tupper Memorial, E. Evans, Cotton St., Raleigh....................	50	75	1:
Union Grove	70	30	1(
Wake Baptist Grove, W. H. Johnson, Garner, R. 2, Box 30	38	60	!
Wake Chapel, Manning Branch, Raleigh, R. 5....................	55	60	11
Wakefield, C. H. High, Zebulon, R. 1, Box 153.....................	107	181	2!
White Oak, Irving Pulley, Spring Hope, N. C., R. 1:...........	20	30	E
Williams Grove, Robert Woods..............................	15	15	!
Woodland Chapel, I. H. Estes, Wake Forest, R. 3...............	30	30	(

LIST OF SUNDAY SCHOOLS

Superintendent and Postoffice	Teachers	Pupils	Total	Co ver
Baptist Grove, D. T. Turner, Raleigh, R. 6....................	3	......	54	
Bethlehem, W. O. Moore, Raleigh, R. 1....................	7	50	57	
Cary Baptist	......	......	......	...
Dawson Street, Raleigh, J. F. Haywood, W. Raleigh	......	......	......	...
Elevation, Lynn Seawell, Raleigh, R. 5....:................	5	60	65	
Elizabeth, N. W. Pulley, Spring Hope, N. C., R. 1........	......	......	30	⌐
Felt's Chapel, W. M. Baker, Louisburg, R. 1................	4	50	54	
First Baptist, Bailey, E. W. Harrison, Bailey..............	......	......	......	...
First Baptist, Franklinton, M. W. Williams..............	11	161	172	1
First Baptist, Fuquay Springs, I. R. Berton, R. 1........	12	175	187	!
First Baptist, Raleigh, M. D. Haywood......................	40	......	1,400	(
First Baptist, Wendell, A. Logan, Wendell..................	3	70	73	1
First Baptist, Wilson, J. Whitefield, Wilson...............	......	......	......	...
First Baptist, Zebulon, W. A. Jones, Zebulon..............	15	45	60	
Fletchers Grove	......	......	......	...
Friendship Chapel, J. Massenburg, Wake Forest, R. 2	4	58	62	:
Gethsemane, J. Jones, Zebulon, R. 2........................	4	96	100	
Good Hope, R. G. Dunn, Raleigh, R. 2......................	8	108	112	!
Hallsville Star	......	......	......	....
Hodges Grove	......	......	......	...
Holly Springs, W. W. Akins, Holly Springs..............	......	......	......	⌐
Jones Chapel, H. Robertson, Knightdale, R. 1, Box 26	4	46	50	
Jones Hill, J. E. Perry, Spring Hope, R. 1................	4	......	70	⌐
Juniper Level, W. G. Walton, McCullers, R. 1............	8	......	157	:
Lovely Hill	......	......	......	...
Macedonia, Richard Pulley, Neuse, R. 2..................	4	53	59	
Malaby's Cross Roads, H. J. Faison, Knightdale, R. 1	......	......	......	...
Mary Grove	......	......	......	...
Martin Street, R. J. Jones, Raleigh........................	14	300	314	:
Mt. Bright, G. C. Feribault, Box 25, Hillsboro...........	......	......	......	!

Superintendent and Postoffice	Teachers	Pupils	Total
Mt. Pleasant (Wake), J. D. Allen,			
Neuse, R. 1, Box 65......................................	4	79	87
Mt. Pleasant (Franklin).....................................	......	......	......
Mt. Zion (Cary), Rev. Willie Smith, West Raleigh....	......	......	......
Mt. Zion (Raleigh), Miss Blanche Lunford, Raleigh..	3	22	25
New Bethel, L. R. Jeffries, Wake Forest, R. 3..............	......	......	......
New Hope, Wm. Vines, Spring Hope............................	4	......	40
New Liberty, Isaac Cook, Louisburg, R. 3.....................	7	......	75
New Light, E. W. Winston, Wake Forest, R. 1...........	4	35	30
New Providence, T. McCullers, Holly Springs, R. 1....	7	......	135
Neuse Sunday School................................	......	......	......
Oak City, T. W. Harris, Method...............................	14	......	109
Oak Grove	......	......	......
Oberlin Baptist, Dr. P. F. Roberts, State College Sta.	12	118	130
Olive Branch, Otha Dunn, Wake Forest P. O............	8	108	116
Open Field	......	......	......
Pilot Baptist, Sidney Jones, Zebulon, R. 2....................	2	50	52
Pleasant Grove, A. Jones, Wendell..............................	......	......	......
Pleasant Hill	......	......	......
River Dell, J. Mills, Raleigh, R. 2............................	......	......	......
Riley Hill, Guyon Perry, Wendell, R. 2, Box 144........	10	100	110
Rocky Spring	......	......	......
Springfield, McKiever Johns, Auburn...........................	9	100	125
South Main Street, W. H. Hawkins, Louisburg..........	11	......	235
Star of Bethlehem	......	......	......
Stokes Chapel, T. S. Stokes, Middlesex.....................	5	......	50
St. Matthews, O. H. Riddick, Neuse, R. 2....................	9	......	94
Tupper Memorial, E. Evans, Raleigh, Cotton St...........	9	85	94
Union Grove, H. B. Wilder, Youngsville.......................	7	75	82
Wake Baptist Grove, M. L. Avery, Garner, R. 2.........	7	79	86
Wake Chapel, J. E. Edgerton, Raleigh, R. 1.................	12	40	47
Wakefield, J. J. High, Zebulon, R. 1..............................	8	120	128
White Oak	......	......	20
Williams Grove, Rev. Wm. Smith, West Raleigh........	......	......	......
Woodland Chapel, R. B. Mangum, Wake Forest, R. 3	4	33	41

B. Y. P. U.'s

Name of President and Postoffice	Membership Male	Female	To:
Bethlehem, E. D. Ray, Raleigh, R. 1	20	25	
Elizabeth	8	15	
Felt's Chapel, W. M. Baker, Louisburg, R. 1	......	......	
First Baptist, Bailey, C. Gilmer, Bailey, R. 1	35	45	
First Baptist, Franklinton, Thomas Glasco, Franklinton....	40	65	1
First Baptist, Fuquay Springs, Miss Maude McKinnzee....	24	27	
First Baptist, Raleigh, C. A. Levister, Raleigh	57	102	1
First Baptist, Zebulon, Mary Christmas, Zebulon	10	8	
Friendship, O. V. Carpenter, Wake Forest	12	18	
Gethsemane, Lizzie Arrington, Zebulon, R. 1	10	16	
Good Hope, C. Watkins, Knightdale, R. 1	......	......	
Jones Hill, R. C. Wheelus, Spring Hope, R. 1	13	20	
Malaby's Cross Roads, Walter Smith, Raleigh, R. 5	12	18	
Martin Street, Raleigh. Aaron Donaldson, S. Haywood St.	......	......	
Mt. Bright, Hillsboro, W. W. Feribault, Hillsboro	10	15 ·	
Mt. Pleasant (Wake), Ralph Justice, Neuse, R. 1	26	34	
New Hope, Miss A. Spivey, Spring Hope	10	12	
New Liberty, Martha E. Perry, Louisburg, R. 3	15	25	
Oak City, Austin Knuckles. Method	15	20	
Olive Branch, William H. Dunston, Wake Forest	20	20	
Pilot, L. G. Heggins, Zebulon, R. 2	9	14	
Pleasant Grove, W. A. Morgan, Wendell	17 .	13	
River Dell	3	9	
Riley Hill, Haywood Horton, Zebulon, R. 3	15	35	
Springfield, Jessie J. Hunter, Auburn	25	35	
South Main Street, Louisburg, D. H. Blount	15	25	
St. Matthews	30	45	
Stokes Chapel, O. Stokes, Middlesex, R. 23	10	15	
Tupper Memorial, Oscar Smith, Raleigh	15	20	
Union Grove, P. E. Yarborough, Youngsville	20	15	
Wake Chapel, Henry Raeford, Jr., Raleigh, R. 1	12	13	
Wake Baptist Grove, T. Palmer, Garner, R. 2	15	25	
Wakefield, Pernell Foster, Zebulon, R. —	10	15	

MINUTES

OF THE

FOURTEENTH ANNUAL SESSION

OF THE

Woman's Auxiliary of the Wake Baptist Association

HELD WITH THE

FELTS CHAPEL BAPTIST CHURCH

NEAR YOUNGSVILLE, N. C.

AUGUST 17-18, 1932

OFFICERS

President, Mrs. B. E. Barrett ....Raleigh
First. Vice-President, Mrs. Armittie Stokes.............'. ..... Middlesex
Recording Secretary, Miss Susan Wilcox..................... ....Method
Assistant Recording Secretary, Mrs. J. A. Gresham ....Zebulon
Corresponding Secretary, Mrs. N. M. Perry........................Wendell
Treasurer, Mrs. N. A. Hunter............. ....Raleigh
Organist, Miss Verdie Parrish..,................. .... Method

---

The next annual session will be held with the Olive Branch
Baptist Church, Wake Forest, N. C., Wednesday before the third
Sunday in August, 1933.

PROCEEDINGS

The Woman's Auxiliary of the Wake Association held its Fourteenth Annual Session at Felts Chapel, near Youngsville, N. C., August 10th, 1932. On Tuesday night at the opening session the service was conducted by Sisters Hunter and Gresham. The opening hymn was "Pass Me Not O Gentle Savior." Scripture reading was taken from the 12th chapter of Hebrews. Prayer by Mrs. N. A. Hunter.

Rev. P. H. Hedgepeth, pastor of Felts Chapel delivered the Welcome Address. Response was made by Miss Susan F. Wilcox.

The program for the first session was rendered by the local church. Rev. John L. Tilley delivered the Annual Sermon. Mr. L. T. Jones made the closing remarks. Collection— $1.05.

WEDNESDAY MORNING SESSION
10:30 A.M.

Praise services were conducted by Sister Caroline Raeford and Sister Riddick, opened with the singing "What A Friend We Have In Jesus." Scripture reading was taken from the Twenty-third Psalm. Hymn: "Jesus, Keep Me Near the Cross."

Following the singing of the above song, the delegates enrolled for the session, and committees were appointed. Miss Lena Marriott read a delightful essay to the body. The subject of the essay was "The Duties of Young Women Who Desire to do Auxiliary Work." The content of her paper was very inspiring and instructive. Mrs. Howell rendered a very delightful solo following the paper by Miss Marriott. Mrs. George S. Stokes made a few brief remarks. Song: "I Am Thine, O Lord." Selection by Mrs. Howell: "Shine for Jesus." Remarks from Mrs. Somerville. Collection— $0.40.

WEDNESDAY AFTERNOON SESSION

Praise services were conducted by Sister Gresham. Miss Verdie Parrish rendered a beautiful vocal solo, "Grateful, O Lord," following the praise services. Mrs. B. E. Barrett, President of the Woman's Auxiliary, delivered the Annual President's Message. The Annual Report of the Corresponding Secretary followed Mrs. Barrett's message. The report was given by the Corresponding Secretary, Mrs. Mamie Perry. Mrs. N. A. Hunter made the report of the Treasurer.

Mrs. Levister delivered a very interesting and instructive talk on the "Church and the Young People." Following this Mrs. Cora Pair Thomas, our missionary to Africa, told of the grave need of more help for Africa and the little value that is put upon the African needs by many of our people here. She stated that many natives have never heard of Christ. While, on the other hand some more advanced in civilization have schools and missions in which they are taught about Jesus Christ. Mrs. Thomas urged us to do our full share of help in the Christian cause to these of Christ's people whom we can help.

After Mrs. Thomas' talk, a beautiful solo was rendered by Mrs. Lillie Finch, "Jesus Met Me There." The meeting then adjourned.

THURSDAY MORNING SESSION

The Thursday session opened with praise service conducted by Sister Annie Freeman and Sister Olivia Jones. Song by audience: "I Will Trust In the Lord." This was followed by prayer by Sister Jones. Mrs. W. C. Somerville read a splendidly prepared paper, "Training Young People Religiously." Mrs. Lizzie B. Foster led the discussion which followed this paper. In the discussion it was stressed upon the congregation the importance of religious training for young people, especially in the present time when religious training is so neglected.

Collection was then taken. Following this the meeting adjourned.

August 18, 1932.

We, your Committee on Officers, recommend the following persons for officers of this Auxiliary for the ensuing year:

PRESIDENT..Mrs. B. E. Barrett
FIRST VICE-PRESIDENT............................. Mrs. Armittie Stokes
RECORDING SECRETARY............................Miss Susan Wilcox
ASSISTANT RECORDING SECRETARY.........Mrs. J. A. Gresham
CORRESPONDING SECRETARY....................Mrs. M. N. Perry
ASSISTANT CORRESPONDING SECRETARY ....
TREASURER..Mrs. N. A. Hunter
ORGANIST..Miss Verdie Parrish

Respectfully submitted,
MRS. ANNIE FREEMAN,
MRS. CAROLINE RAEFORD,
MISS LENA F. MARRIOTT,
Committee.

FINANCIAL REPORT

EXTRA SESSION ....$ 27.55
ANNUAL SESSION... 39.65
PUBLIC COLLECTION.. 4.35
                                                                        ————
    TOTAL...$ 71.55

20 garments were turned over to the Auxiliary by members. Turned over to the Wake Association for Annual Sitting— $44.00.

Lightning Source UK Ltd.
Milton Keynes UK
UKHW022320211118
332685UK00005B/156/P